100
JUMPERS TO FOLLOW 2020–21

Fifty-nineth year of publication

Edited by James de Wesselow

Contributors:

Mark Boylan
Marcus Buckland
Rodney Pettinga
James Stevens
David Toft
Richard Young

RACING POST

Commissioned by RACING POST, Floor 7, Vivo Building South Bank
Central, 30 Stamford Street, London, SE1 9LS

First published in 2020 by PITCH PUBLISHING Ltd
A2 Yeoman Gate, Yeoman Way, Worthing, Sussex, BN13 3QZ
Order line: 01933 304 858

ISBN 978-1-78531-831-3

Printed and bound in Great Britain by Pureprint

100 WINNERS

JUMPERS TO FOLLOW 2020-21

(ages as at 2020)

ABACADABRAS (FR) 6 b g

Supporters of Abacadabras were dealt a cruel blow at the start of the 2020 Cheltenham Festival when the smart Gigginstown runner got collared late by Shishkin in the Supreme Novices' Hurdle. It was far from a straightforward run as he started slowly before a faller caused some issues. However, he travelled into the race with a real amount of class. He looks the sort to continue to progress into this campaign. Prior to the festival, he was an eight-length winner of the Grade 1 Paddy Power Future Champions Novice Hurdle, which highlights his talent, and we think he looks primed to make a big impact in the Champion Hurdle division this season. He is a seriously high-class and speedy hurdler who should have more to offer this campaign. GORDON ELLIOTT

AJERO (IRE) 5 b g

This Red Jazz gelding had future winner written all over him when finishing an eyecatching third in a Thurles bumper last February for trainer Tom Mullins and it's interesting to see he's since joined the much-respected Kim Bailey team. Ridden by Jamie Codd on his debut, the half-brother to Bailey's high-class Charbel looked green under pressure but came home very nicely. He shouldn't have to wait long to make an impact over hurdles in Britain and it's likely he will have plenty of improvement to come both from a mental and physical perspective. A lovely prospect. KIM BAILEY

ALLAHO (FR) 6 b g

Allaho has all the hallmarks of maintaining his status as a top prospect. He had one unsuccessful run in a bumper on his opening start for Willie Mullins but was pitched into Grade 3 company and stepped up to 3m on his first hurdling start, which he won, and then ran with credit in a couple of top-flight contests in just two more outings that campaign. It wasn't a too dissimilar path as a chaser last season, for although he didn't win first time up over fences, he did win when next seen and then ran really well in the RSA Chase to secure third. That was just his eighth start so, with age clearly on his side, he can get even better with experience and become a serious Ryanair or Gold Cup candidate come March. WILLIE MULLINS.

AN FRAOCH MOR (IRE) 7 b g

We surely haven't yet seen the best of this unexposed chaser and there's every chance he could be set for a very fruitful 2020-21 campaign. This likeable seven-year-old was a capable hurdler, rated 120 in that sphere, but looked an improved performer over fences, catching the eye when second to Debuchet at Fairyhouse before winning readily at Naas last winter. He proved disappointing as the 11-2 favourite for a competitive Grade B handicap chase at Naas when last seen in February but had the excuse of an overreach on his right fore, as well as losing a shoe. We expect him to bounce back in a big way this season. ROSS O'SULLIVAN

APPRECIATE IT (Ire) 6 b g

One of the leading bumper horses of last season, he has endless potential now switching to hurdles. Having looked the real deal when winning twice at Leopardstown either side of Christmas, most notably when cruising clear in a Grade 2 in February, he went to the Cheltenham Festival with a huge reputation and had a legion of supporters in the Grade 1 Champion Bumper, only to find stablemate Ferny Hollow too speedy in the final furlong. He travelled like the winner for much of the way, however, and being a half-brother to 2m4f-2m6f hurdle winner Pilgrim Way and point and useful bumper winner Danny Kirwan, he ought to improve for longer trips over hurdles this season. WILLIE MULLINS

BALLYADAM (IRE) 5 b g

A four-length winner on his only pointing start in a 3m 4yo race, Ballyadam was purchased for £330,000 the following month by new connections. Clearly expectations were going to be high when he made his rules debut and he was a 1-4 shot. He travelled in behind like a superstar but the heavy ground, after racing keenly, just caught him out and third was the best he could do. However, in less-demanding conditions next time he showed what he's all about, this time being sent off 1-6 and forged 18 lengths clear on his nearest pursuer. Novice hurdles surely await him now and there's every chance he'll be among the best of that group come April. GORDON ELLIOTT.

BOB OLINGER (IRE) 5 b g

Henry de Bromhead looks to have a seriously exciting prospect on his hands in the shape of this wide-margin Gowran bumper winner last March. But for Covid-19's racing shutdown, this young talent could well have been a major player in either of the major Aintree or Punchestown festival bumpers. A 15 length point-to-point winner on debut last November, the Sholokhov gelding was privately purchased by Brian Acheson's Robcour ownership vehicle and couldn't have been more impressive on his sole run under rules, toying with a well-regarded 12 length point-to-point winner. He should prove one of his trainer's leading novice hurdlers this term. HENRY DE BROMHEAD

BOOTHILL (IRE) 5 bb g

Harry Fry is renowned for not rushing his horses and patience will be key for Boothill, who has reportedly had a couple of minor setbacks and is unlikely to be seen until the second half of the season. And we think there's plenty to look forward to as the scopey son of Presenting, who shaped well in two Irish points in 2019, created a really good impression when winning a traditionally strong Kempton bumper in good fashion on his debut under rules in February. There's plenty of stamina in his pedigree and this highly regarded sort is one to keep a close eye out for in novice hurdles over 2m4f and beyond. HARRY FRY

BREWIN'UPASTORM (IRE) 7yo b g

Olly Murphy's leading prospect still has a huge future ahead of him over fences after three highly promising efforts last season. He won stylishly in a red-hot novice chase at Carlisle on his debut, beating Good Boy Bobby and two subsequent Grade 2 winners, Midnight Shadow and Global Citizen. Murphy claimed his runner was not 100 percent that day, and we probably still haven't seen the best from Barbara Hester's seven-year-old. In the Arkle, he was beginning to edge closer to the leaders before unseating Richard Johnson four from home, although his jumping that day was far from perfect. There is plenty of potential to exploit his mark of 150, but it would be no surprise if Brewin'Upastorm is pitched back at Graded level with connections looking to gauge whether he could emerge as a Champion Chase contender. OLLY MURPHY

CAPTAIN GUINNESS (IRE) 5 b g

It would be no surprise if this extremely talented youngster developed into one of the leading novice chasing prospects for the 2020-21 campaign, with the 20-1 on offer for the Arkle Novices' Chase of some appeal even at this early stage in proceedings. The Arakan gelding's raw ability saw him defy his inexperience when winning on his debut at Navan in December, and he was arguably the horse to note from the Moscow Flyer Novice Hurdle despite being just touched off by Andy Dufresne. He was by no means a spent force when being brought down at the second last in the Supreme Novices' Hurdle and should have a fair deal of improvement to come. We believe he's a surefire winner this season. HENRY DE BROMHEAD

CAPTAIN KANGAROO (IRE) 5 ch g

Captain Kangaroo is definitely one of the most unexposed horses in the Willie Mullins yard. He never ran for John Hammond on the Flat in France, but it would have been interesting to see how he'd have fared considering his siblings include lightly raced Group 3 winner Sky Kingdom. That trainer's loss was his new stable's gain and he immediately made a big impact when landing a 2m2.5f soft-ground Clonmel bumper, with the third that day already landing a maiden hurdle subsequently (RPR 138 at the time of this book's publication). He's sure to be placed to his best advantage in the coming season, whether he stays in National Hunt Flat races or heads over hurdles. WILLIE MULLINS.

CASTRA VETERA (IRE) 5 b m

Considering the promise that this sizeable mare showed in bumpers last season, it would be disappointing if she didn't have a pretty significant campaign ahead over hurdles – especially when competing against her own sex. This daughter of Jeremy had her only blip last term when performing below expectations in the Grade 2 mares' bumper at the Dublin Racing Festival, but the ground was surely quicker than ideal for her on that occasion and her inexperience may have counted against her. It was reassuring to see her get back to winning ways at Naas in March and she is in the right hands to improve her two from three record. JOSEPH O'BRIEN

CEDARWOOD ROAD (IRE) 5 b g

This likeable Stowaway gelding has been brought along very gradually by the Gearoid O'Loughlin team and there's every chance connections can reap the benefits of that campaign this season over fences. An eyecatcher on his hurdles debut at Fairyhouse in November, the Chris Jones-owned performer rewarded good market support when bolting up in a traditionally strong maiden hurdle at the Leopardstown Christmas festival and confirmed his class when plundering a Listed contest in March at Naas. With physical improvement to come, he could develop into a very useful novice chaser this season. A beginners' chase success should be a formality somewhere along the way. GEAROID O'LOUGHLIN

CHACUN POUR SOI (FR) 8 b g

It was a cruel blow to this massively talented chaser that he missed out on his intended run in last season's Queen Mother Champion Chase with a foot abscess at the 11th hour. Considering how the race unfolded, with Altior also missing the race and Defi Du Seuil failing to fire, he surely would have had a huge impact if making it to the track that day. He oozed class

in his Grade 1 win over stablemate Min at the Dublin Racing
Festival prior to that, and with last season's Arkle Novices' Chase
failing to really throw up a star contender for the senior 2m
chasing division, the Susannah Ricci-owned performer should be
set for a profitable time of things. WILLIE MULLINS

CHAMP (IRE) 8 b g

Nicky Henderson has strong claims of lifting the Cheltenham
Gold Cup trophy for a third time with his current hand of
Champ and Santini. The last-named is a high-class sort but
it's Champ that appeals most for the festival showpiece and
he's worth an early interest at a best-priced 12-1 at the time of
writing. This dual Grade 1 winning hurdler has improved with
every start over fences and made up a considerable amount
of ground in the home straight to win this year's RSA (which
looked a strong renewal) in March. There's certainly room for
improvement in the jumping department but he's in the right
hands to iron out any blemishes and the Gold Cup trip of 3m2f
will be ideal. NICKY HENDERSON

CHAMPAGNE COURT (IRE) 7 b g

A switch to fences was always going to suit Champagne Court
and he rewarded connections with two wins over the big
obstacles. He has posted smart form throughout his career,
notably at Cheltenham, finishing fourth in a strong bumper
in October, and also at the 2019 festival. When chasing in late
2019 he won good races at Sandown and Plumpton in impressive
fashion before posting two solid runs in Cheltenham's two novice
handicap chases in January and at the 2020 festival. He was
beaten 21 lengths in both races but travelled well, before not
finding the extra gear required. A stiffer test on soft ground is
bound to suit him as he ages and he would be well-treated off a
mark of 141. He can take in one of the many top 3m handicaps
throughout the season. JEREMY SCOTT

CHAMPAGNESUPEROVER (IRE) 5 b g

Few horses win races in the manner that Champagnesuperover did when thrashing his rivals with his rider sitting motionless throughout on his debut in a soft-ground Ayr bumper in January. And although the form behind the winner is ordinary, punters saw fit to make him favourite for a Listed contest at Newbury on his only subsequent outing. The quicker conditions coupled with a steady gallop found him out and he could only manage third place that day, but he remains a horse of considerable potential and he'll stay a fair bit further than 2m when he tackles obstacles. We think he's a very exciting prospect. OLLY MURPHY

CHANTRY HOUSE (IRE) 6 br g

One would expect Nicky Henderson to take this exciting prospect chasing this season, where he can build on a highly promising start to his career. A £295,000 purchase, Chantry House won his bumper and first two novice hurdles really stylishly – and beat some good horses in the process – before running a fine third in the Supreme Novices' Hurdle. Considering he was a 3m point-to-point winner, that effort highlights his natural class and a stiffer test and going over fences will bring out much more improvement next season. Expect him to be campaigned at around 2m4f and perhaps later in the season he can emerge as the stable's Scilly Isles horse, a race his trainer always targets. NICKY HENDERSON

CHRIS'S DREAM (IRE) 8 b g

He may have been safely held in last season's Magners Cheltenham Gold Cup, but that doesn't mean this likeable chaser isn't up to Grade 1 standard and he should be able to show his true ability this season – especially when the mud is flying. The Mahler gelding made a mockery of his mark of 146 when bolting up in the Troytown Chase at Navan on his seasonal bow and was primed for a tilt at the Irish Gold Cup before drying ground saw him withdrawn. The improving eight-year-old claimed the Grade 2 Red Mills Chase at Gowran in February and tends to be at his best fresh. We expect him to collect in the early stages of the season. HENRY DE BROMHEAD

CLONDAW CAITLIN (IRE) 5 b m

Ruth Jefferson has inherited plenty of her late father Malcolm's traits and the 'old man' would have approved of her handling of Clondaw Caitlin, who won four of her five starts last season and is unbeaten over hurdles. Although down in trip, there was plenty to like about the way she won a Grade 2 at Kelso on her final start and, as she was only raised 2lb, her current BHA mark of 135 will make her of interest in handicaps, the return to 2m4f will suit, she's open to improvement and she has the option of contesting the less-competitive mares' races. She has the physique of one that should be equally adept over fences. RUTH JEFFERSON

COEUR SUBLIME (IRE) 5 b g

It will be interesting to see if a change of scenery from Gordon Elliott to Gearoid O'Loughlin can see this talented five-year-old show his full potential this season, having proved disappointing when last seen in this year's Champion Hurdle behind Epatante. The 2019 Triumph Hurdle runner-up began last season with a bang when bolting up in the WKD Hurdle at Down Royal but apparently made a noise when third to Sharjah at Leopardstown in December, later undergoing a breathing procedure. It appears as though he is one who has often shown plenty in his homework and should have more to offer on the track. GEAROID O'LOUGHLIN

CONCERTISTA (FR) 6 ch m

Successful on the Flat over 1m2f in her native France in May 2017, this daughter of Nathaniel missed all of 2018 through injury after joining current connections for €75,000. She's made up for lost time since, however. She was short-headed on her hurdling debut in the Grade 2 Mares' Novices' Hurdle at the Cheltenham Festival in March 2019 before going one better in the same race 12 months later when bounding clear 12 lengths under Daryl Jacob. Now officially rated 148, she remains lightly raced and looks capable of adding a valuable Grade 1 win to her name in the upcoming campaign. WILLIE MULLINS

CONFIRMATION BIAS (IRE) 5 b g

There was plenty to like about how this €150,000 three-year-old purchase shaped in two bumpers last year, and he should have little trouble making his presence felt over hurdles this season for leading connections. The fact he was able to come out on top in a Wincanton bumper last November, despite showing plenty of greenness, suggested he has an above-average level of ability and he shouldn't be judged too harshly on his defeat at the same venue in December to Supamouse (who would have been a leading Champion Bumper contender but for his sad passing). Provided he jumps adequately, there should be races to be won this season. PAUL NICHOLLS

COPPERHEAD 6 ch g

One of the highlights in last season's novice chase department was Copperhead's demolition of hitherto-unbeaten chaser Two For Gold in the Reynoldstown at Ascot in February. It was hard not to be impressed with the way Colin Tizzard's six-year-old travelled and jumped before pulling clear in the home straight to win by 17 lengths. He failed to match that for whatever reason in the RSA, beaten when falling at the last at Cheltenham, but he's in very good hands and can put that firmly behind him this season. We think the Ladbrokes Trophy at Newbury in November looks an obvious early-season target, for which, at the time of writing he's currently available around 14-1. COLIN TIZZARD

COQUELICOT (FR) 4 bb f

This likeable mare finished second on her first two starts in junior bumpers last season but she was able to take her form to a new level when stepping up to 2m, winning all of her remaining three starts at the distance. A winner on heavy ground at Taunton in January, she showed her versatility in terms of ground when following up under a penalty at Huntingdon the next month on good to soft, prior to completing her hat-trick in Listed company at Kempton in March. She was still notably green when out in front on the last of those victories, so it's quite possible there will be plenty more improvement to come from her now she's switching to hurdles. ANTHONY HONEYBALL

CORNERSTONE LAD 6 b g

A dual winner on the Flat at a modest level up to 2m, this gelding has improved out of all recognition since switching codes and hit the headlines last season when accounting for Champion Hurdler Buveur D'Air in the Grade 1 Fighting Fifth at Newcastle in heavy going in November 2019. A real mudlark, he showed that form was no fluke when running to the same RPR of 159 when a close third in the Grade 2 Champion Hurdle Trial at Haydock on his next start in January. Having improved by around 20lb since the start of the season, he may have been over the top when running disappointingly in the Champion Hurdle itself at Cheltenham in March. He has the option of staying over hurdles or going novice chasing. MICKY HAMMOND

DANNY WHIZZBANG (IRE) 7 b g

This fine son of Getaway never quite built on the big promise he showed on his chasing bow last season but remains open to plenty of improvement in handicaps this term. The Paul Nicholls-trained seven-year-old was a comfortable winner of the Grade 2 race at Newbury's Ladbrokes Trophy meeting. He defeated Reserve Tank in good style that day, which looks solid form, even if he did only beat two runners. But he struggled in two starts after, finishing well-beaten in the Kauto Star and Reynoldstown next and struggling in a race at Ascot. Another year to develop, a more prolonged campaign and tackling handicaps with more emphasis on stamina and we think we should see him in a better light this season. He's one to watch off a mark of 145. PAUL NICHOLLS

DARVER STAR (IRE) 8 b g

This extremely talented performer was one of the standout stories of last season in Ireland, showing incredible improvement after being beaten in a Wexford maiden hurdle (when rated 104) to finishing third to Epatante in the Champion Hurdle at Cheltenham. The Irish Champion Hurdle runner-up has always given the impression he'll be an even better chaser and he rates one of the most exciting hurdlers to be heading over fences this term. Gavin Cromwell is a master at placing his horses and should be able to build his confidence for a potential tilt at next year's Arkle Novices' Chase at Cheltenham. GAVIN CROMWELL

DEISE ABA (IRE) 7 b g

It looks significant that owner Trevor Hemmings, who sold over 60 percent of his horses at the September dispersal sale, has kept hold of the very useful second-season chaser Deise Aba. This Irish point and hurdle winner confirmed stamina was his forte, as his pedigree suggested, when winning chases at

Catterick and Sandown (handicap) early in 2020 and, although only fifth, he ran to his best when staying-on fifth to Milan Native in the Kim Muir at the festival. As a lightly raced sort he's open to plenty of improvement this season and the demands of the Welsh National in December should see him in a favourable light. PHILIP HOBBS

EASYSLAND (FR) 6 b g
Purchased by JP McManus in January, this prolific cross-country winner showed it was money very well spent when he recorded one of the most impressive performances at last season's Cheltenham Festival in March, beating reigning champion and dual Grand National hero Tiger Roll by an incredible 17 lengths. He became the owner's seventh winner of the Glenfarclas Chase at the festival and, given he's only six, he could be something of a standing dish in the event for a few years to come. DAVID COTTIN

ELFILE (FR) 6 b m
Owner Kenny Alexander is building quite the band of talented mares and this 151-rated hurdler should be set for a big season over fences, while Honeysuckle, owned by the same connections, remains hurdling. The Willie Mullins-trained French recruit has ended up somewhat in Honeysuckle's shadow over hurdles, second to that rival in a Fairyhouse Grade 1 in April 2019 and third behind the Irish Champion Hurdle heroine in the Mares' Hurdle at Cheltenham last March. Provided she takes to fences well, there should be a number of good Graded opportunities for her to capitalise on this term. WILLIE MULLINS

ELIXIR D'AINAY (FR) 6 ch g
Although Elixir D'Ainay's wins have been in a French bumper and a maiden hurdle at Naas, the progressive six-year-old has

shown smart form in defeat. Finishing second to potential top-notcher Envoi Allen at the highest level in January rates a career-best effort and, although he was down markedly in distance, he was in the process of running well when knocked over at the penultimate hurdle of the Supreme Novice. Given he stays further than two miles coupled with the way he was travelling it's safe to assume that he'd have been among the placings without that mishap. He's the type to make his mark in Graded company this term. WILLIE MULLINS

EMITOM (IRE) 6 b g

Warren Greatrex has always held this horse in high regard and towards the end of last season he proved exactly what he was capable of. He ran no race on his return but bounced back with an impressive eight-length success in the Rendlesham. That was far from a strong race for a Grade 2, but the manner in which he raced and then kicked clear was striking. In the Stayers' Hurdle he finished a decent fourth, when he hit a hurdle and was much less experienced than his rivals. He may also be better suited to a flat track. Chasing is on the agenda now, which should suit, and if he can continue on his upward curve he could mix it with the best in that division. There is much more to come from this horse, who has a proper stamp of class about him. WARREN GREATREX

ENRILO (FR) 6 bl g

The best days of Enrilo's career were always expected to come over fences so it will be interesting to see what he can do in a likely novice chase campaign this season. He boasted good form in bumpers and won over hurdles highlighted by his Grade 2 Winter Novices' Hurdle success at Sandown. He showed a really good attitude to win that day. Although he was tried again on soft ground when a lengthy third in the Challow at Newbury, the better ground could bring about more improvement this campaign. He did not race again after his Grade 1 third, with connections most likely waiting for spring ground and keen to get him in peak shape for this season. He has the scope to go far over fences and his form so far suggests he could be a leading player over 2m4f and possibly a little bit further. PAUL NICHOLLS

ENVOI ALLEN (FR) 6 b g

It'll come as no great surprise to learn that Envoi Allen has been featured in this book for the last two years considering it's all about highlighting winners. It's true to say you won't have got rich from backing him. He mostly picked up his races as an odds-on shot, but the fact he went off a 4-7 chance to land the Ballymore Novices' Hurdle in March on his final outing of last season eloquently shows just how classy this gelding is. There had been talk in early 2020 that the gelding could possibly head to the Champion Hurdle, such was the belief in him by his connections, but they kept him with the novices. All options are open but it's expected that he'll at least try fences this winter. GORDON ELLIOTT.

ERIC BLOODAXE (IRE) 5 bl g

Expect this high-class former bumper to develop into one of Joseph O'Brien's top novice hurdlers this season. He looked an extremely bright prospect when winning his first two starts last winter. Subsequent Champion Bumper scorer Ferny Hollow was behind the Gigginstown-owned performer at Fairyhouse in December, while he beat a smart sort in the shape of Wide Receiver on his second start at Leopardstown later that month. We clearly didn't see the real Eric Bloodaxe at the Dublin Racing Festival when he returned lame, but he gives the impression he's one to improve after his summer's break. JOSEPH O'BRIEN

EVERGLOW 5 br g

It may be that Everglow will be seen to best effect when sent chasing and tested over a longer trip, but he could certainly scoop some nice prizes in novice hurdling company before that test. He is a maiden after two bumper runs but there was plenty to like about his start to life. He was a neck second in a hot race at Chepstow, travelling like the best horse in the race but just lacking the speed in the final stages. He was upped to Listed level next, finishing third in a very strong race at Cheltenham's November meeting behind the high-class Israel Champ and odds-on favourite Time Flies By. That was a great run but again he just lacked the required speed in the closing stages. He has been crying out for a longer trip, which he will get over hurdles. He is a strong travelling quality horse with a big future ahead over the next few years; soft ground should be ideal. PHILIP HOBBS

FAKIR D'OUDAIRIES (FR) 5 b g

There's little doubting that this JP McManus-owned performer was a talented hurdler but he took his form to a whole new level over fences last season and, being just a five-year-old, there could be more to come from him this season. A mistake at the second last in the Arkle Novices' Chase came at a crucial time against the likeable Put The Kettle On, but he still rallied gamely for second. When the ground is at its most testing, this battle-hardened youngster is very effective and while he may not have the star quality of Chacun Pour Soi or Defi Du Seuil, there are certainly Graded races to be won with him this winter. JOSEPH O'BRIEN

FAROUK D'ALENE (FR) 5 b g

Farouk D'alene has been to the sales' a few times. On the second occasion, May 2018, he was purchased for 34,000gns, with the gelding still to make the racetrack. There isn't anything overly compelling about his pedigree so he must have been showing something at home or been growing into a nice type. However, the next time he found a new home was after his 18 lengths' success in a 3m soft-ground four-year-old maiden point, with current connections going to £260,000 at Cheltenham's Festival Sale to land him. He immediately paid a tiny chunk of his price tag off when making all on his rules debut for an easy victory, and then recovered a bit more of his purchase price when winning all out to follow up from another nice type, handing that rival 3lb in the process. Everything points to this son of Racinger being a top novice during the 2020-21 season. GORDON ELLIOTT.

FELIX DESJY (FR) 7 ch g

The Galway Hurdle turned into a nightmare for this former Grade 1-winning novice hurdler but he should have little trouble getting back on track this winter, remaining a bright prospect for the Gordon Elliott team. We didn't get to see him again last season, having come fifth in the Supreme Novices' Hurdle in 2019 but he appeared to be close to returning last spring and his Flat comeback at Navan was very pleasing, blitzing the field by eight lengths in a maiden. His trainer is renowned for placing horses to good effect and it would be disappointing if this very capable operator didn't return to the winner's enclosure over the coming months. GORDON ELLIOTT

FERNY HOLLOW (IRE) 5 bb g

This gelding took the National Hunt game by storm last season when defeating his heavily backed stablemate Appreciate It in the Champion Bumper at Cheltenham in March, following in the hoofprints of Envoi Allen, who'd won the race the previous year for the same owners, Cheveley Park Stud. A winning pointer at four, he was beaten on his first two outings in bumpers, but hasn't looked back since having a hood applied, recording hugely impressive RPRs of 136 and 141 in his two victories at Fairyhouse and Cheltenham. A strong-looking son of Westerner, he relishes testing ground and could be capable of absolutely anything tackling hurdles. WILLIE MULLINS

FLIGHT DECK (IRE) 6 b g

Although one of the stable's lesser lights, the unexposed Flight Deck will be interesting in mid-range handicaps over either hurdles or fences in the coming months. Following three inauspicious runs at big prices in novice/maiden company in the 2018-19 season, the six-year-old reappeared after a 400-day absence and showed considerable improvement to win at single-figure odds on his handicap debut in a 2m4f soft-ground Newbury hurdle in February. That form worked out really well and, assuming he stays sound, he'll be one to look out for, especially as he goes up again in distance. He'll reportedly go over fences sooner rather than later. JONJO O'NEILL

FLINTEUR SACRE (FR) 5 b g

Nicky Henderson has a lot of exciting novice hurdlers having their first starts in the coming months. Flinteur Sacre is probably the one who'll garner the most attention in that company considering he's a brother to the brilliant Sprinter Sacre. At a time when hundreds of thousands of pounds is spent on National Hunt horses, he wasn't the most expensive purchase at €125,000 as a two-year-old, considering the pedigree. Of course he was never going to be seen on the track at that age and he made his debut in a bumper, as a five-year-old, at Newbury. He claimed second that day in heavy ground but then went on to shed his maiden status at Kempton on a quicker surface in impressive style. Any thoughts of going to the Champion Bumper were quickly dismissed due to the pandemic and his return to the track is greatly anticipated. NICKY HENDERSON.

FULGURIX (FR) 5 br g

An interesting ex-French-trained gelding joining the Colin Tizzard Team this season is Fulgurix, who is one of a couple of horses sent to him by Simon Munir and Isaac Souede. The form of his sole previous outing, which came at Pau in December 2019, a race in which the aforementioned owners had the winner, may not work out to be above average, but what was noticeable about him during the contest was his size. He was much bigger and more robust than many of his rivals. Therefore, it's exciting that he was pretty much the last one off the bridle before fading to the winner late on, the pair miles clear of the remainder. Having had a nice long time to acclimatise to his new surroundings and grow more into his frame connections should be rewarded at least once during his novice season. COLIN TIZZARD.

GETAROUND (IRE) 5 gr g

Ella Pickard has made a good start to her training career and Getaround looks likely to fly the flag for the stable this season. The five-year-old has won a point-to-point, bumper and is now unbeaten in two starts over hurdles for the stable. He beat some decent types in a front-running 14-length demolition at Exeter in March before backing that up with a comfortable win at Perth. He set a fair pace up front, jumped pretty well and won in the manner his 2-5 odds suggested, setting up a tilt at the Persian War as an early-season target. A longer trip and softer ground is bound to suit him more than conditions in Scotland and it will be interesting to see how he fares with those solid hurdling runs in the book. Another who will be fascinating when sent chasing too. ELLA PICKARD

GOSHEN (FR) 4 b g

Every year there'll be many unlucky losers in various sports across the world, but Goshen's unseat when about to impressively land the Triumph Hurdle ranks somewhere near the top of 2020's list. He didn't show a great deal on his first three Flat starts in 2018 but then started on a roll of success that saw him win three times before going over hurdles. His opening effort over timber was spectacular from the front, which is his trademark, and he built on this with a 34-length success at Sandown under a penalty before pulling 11 lengths clear of his rivals at Ascot under a double penalty. What happened 55 days later at Cheltenham still beggars belief; the gelding pretty much tripped himself up at the final hurdle when around ten lengths clear. He returned to action on the Flat in September and was below his best, but he should still be a top force in 2m Graded races this campaign. GARY MOORE.

GREANETEEN (FR) 6yo b g

Paul Nicholls has won the Queen Mother Champion Chase three times this century with French-breds and, although he needs to improve a fair bit to emulate those horses, fellow countryman Greaneteen looks just the type to make up into a good-quality 2m chaser this season. The six-year-old created a favourable impression when winning his first three chases but he ran his best race, in terms of form, when fourth in the Johnny Henderson at the festival. He has reportedly done well since and the Haldon Gold Cup at Exeter in November, a race his stable have won twice in the last five years, looks a good starting point. PAUL NICHOLLS

GYPSY ISLAND (IRE) 6 b m

One of the most exciting bumper mares in recent seasons, this ultra-talented daughter of Jeremy was antepost favourite for the Dawn Run Mares' Novices' Hurdle before missing the entire

campaign due to a small fracture on a hind leg in November. It
came as a massive blow to her extremely capable handler Peter
Fahey, but the JP McManus-owned mare should be able to
make up for lost time this term and can create a big splash in
the mares' novice hurdling division. The only mare to beat her
in her five-race career is Arkle heroine Put The Kettle On and
her winning form looks rock solid. PETER FAHEY

HARRY SENIOR (IRE) 6 b g
It took Colin Tizzard a few runs to work out how best to
campaign Harry Senior and a step up in distance proved the
key with two impressive back-to-back novice hurdle wins.
He quickened smartly to win at Chepstow before following
up in excellent fashion in the Grade 2 Ballymore trial at
Cheltenham. He came from off the pace and galloped home
in good fashion to beat serious opposition; it suggested a step
up in trip would bring further improvement. That did not
quite happen when he was pulled-up in the Albert Bartlett but
that was more likely a reflection of the stable's disappointing
form during festival week. His pedigree suggests the switch to
chasing will suit and he looks one to follow over 3m on winter
ground. COLIN TIZZARD

HOLD THE NOTE (IRE) 6 b g
Mick Channon may have been dealt a blessing in disguise in
that Hold The Note did not win his four starts last season and
as such preserves his novice chase status. His form, however,
looks very good. He was unlucky to get collared late in the
Hampton Novices' Chase at Warwick by Two For Gold who
was prolific over fences last year. Hold The Note finished
the season with an excellent third in the novice handicap at
the festival – a race connections previously won with Mister

Whitaker – and he is only 1lb higher for that bold effort behind two well fancied rivals. A return to that festival contest looks the obvious target but he could make an impact in the plethora of 2m4f handicap targets before then or go into Graded novice company. MICK CHANNON

HOLLOW GAMES (IRE) 4 b g

Trainer Gordon Elliott has a very good record with expensive purchases from the pointing field with the likes of Samcro, Envoi Allen and Ballyadam all recent examples. Therefore, the fact that Hollow Games went to the top Irish handler for £255,000 four days after his 30-length four-year-old maiden point success can be seen as a big positive. It's reasonably fair to say that his pedigree isn't the most exciting, as there is only one winner among his siblings, so his value has to be more about his talent, which he clearly displayed at Turtulla that day, pulling well away. Given his age it remains to be seen how much racing he'll have in bumpers considering he had plenty of time to mature, but one win at least in them seems assured. GORDON ELLIOTT.

I K BRUNEL 6 b g

Olly Murphy, who has come a long way in a short time in the training ranks, has a very interesting first-season chaser in I K Brunel. This bumper winner notched his second hurdle victory and turned in a very useful performance when beating previous wide-margin scorer Saint Xavier when upped to 3m at Musselburgh in February. And, although touched off by a more experienced chaser on his first run over fences at Fontwell in early October, the gelding jumped soundly in the main and showed more than enough to suggest he should be able to win in this new sphere, especially when he returns to 3m. OLLY MURPHY

ITCHY FEET (FR) 6 b g

A winner of a Listed hurdle at Kempton two years ago and
third in the 2019 Supreme Novices' Hurdle behind Klassical
Dream, he ran only once over hurdles last season prior to
embarking on a novice chase campaign. Barely breaking
sweat to beat two rivals on his chase debut at Leicester over
Christmas, he made light of his lack of chasing experience
when providing his trainer with a first Grade 1 success when
landing the Scilly Isles Novices' Chase at Sandown on his next
start. Sent-off just 7-2 for the Grade 1 Marsh Novices' Chase
at the Cheltenham Festival subsequently, he looked well
beforehand but made early mistakes and paid the price when
unshipping his rider at the sixth. He'll hopefully have learnt
from that and looks set for a big second season over fences.
OLLY MURPHY

JON SNOW (FR) 5 br g

Useful in a handful of starts on the Flat in France, Jon Snow
had 544 days off before making his debut for Willie Mullins.
It is reasonably fair to say he was a little disappointing early
on for new connections considering there was a bit of a buzz
about him prior to his hurdling debut. He picked up his
first win in an ordinary maiden in early 2020 before having
a break. A return to the Flat in June didn't yield a great
performance but it did serve to sharpen him up, and when
sent back jumping it saw him gain back-to-back victories in
late summer, gaining significant new RPRs; one was 150 when
sent right up in distance to 2m7f. This shows that the hype
which surrounded him at one point may now start to show
itself on the track having unlocked his staying potential.
WILLIE MULLINS.

KID COMMANDO 6 b g

Anthony Honeyball thinks the world of this six-year-old,
who is expected to be given a campaign over fences this

year, a sphere he is destined to shine in. He rose through the ranks quite quickly last year, winning a bumper in impressive fashion at Fontwell and a maiden hurdle at Plumpton. He ran a respectable race on his first test at Graded level, finishing a seven-and-a-half length third in the Dovecote Novices' Hurdle. He had some excuses that day too, as he did not settle as well as his rivals, but he moved into the race well and stayed on in good style. The ground may have been on the quick side too. We think Kid Commando should improve now going over fences and will be seen to best effect on softer ground. ANTHONY HONEYBALL

KILLER KANE (IRE) 5 b g

It doesn't always follow that if a horse has a high-class sibling he or she will end up being one as well, but it does happen. Killer Kane is a prime candidate to uphold the family honour. He's a half-brother to Noel Meade's triple Grade 1 winner Go Native, so if the dam has passed on some of that ability, new connections should have a lot of fun with this son of Oscar. Before he even ran he went through the sales for €70,000 and just under two years later he won a 2m maiden point at Ballycahane. Five days later he visited the sales and got purchased for £300,000. His new trainer has acquired a gelding that has all the ingredients to be a top-flight performer. COLIN TIZZARD

KING ROLAND (IRE) 6 br g

This son of Stowaway has been a bit of a talking horse ever since his emphatic first win for Harry Fry at Uttoxeter. A lot was expected of him in his novice hurdling campaign and, while he did not quite sparkle, there was plenty to take from his three starts. He finished a good second in a strong race at Newbury; he obliged in a weaker race at Exeter before settling for the runner-up spot again in the Ballymore trial at Cheltenham, beaten by another smart prospect in Harry Senior. Sean Bowen reported he was too free in that race but it is hard to be certain he stayed the 2m4½f. Another year to develop will do him the world of good and, if he has strengthened, he should be able to get trips up to 2m5f. Novice chasing looks the obvious route, although connections could look to exploit a mark of 140. HARRY FRY

L'AIR DU VENT (FR) 6 b g

A big season was expected of L'Air Du Vent last season, although he never quite built on the promise he showed when a rare bumper winner for Colin Tizzard in April 2019. His best effort, however, came on his hurdling bow when running a huge race at Cheltenham's October meeting to finish a close third. His jumping that day was mixed, as expected of a horse with little experience, but he showed enough to suggest he was up to winning a good prize. He ran no race in a good contest at Newbury next, and finished tired when fifth behind the classy Chantry House. He had excuses that day, having undergone wind surgery and he had a tongue-tie for the first time. He could take a big step forward when sent chasing and may finally live up to his lofty reputation this season. COLIN TIZZARD

LANGER DAN (IRE) 4 b g

Given there's plenty of stamina in his pedigree, Langer Dan deserves credit for winning twice over 2m at Ludlow and at Wetherby and similarly when finishing sixth after meeting trouble at a crucial stage on his handicap debut in the competitive Boodles Juvenile Hurdle (previously the Fred Winter) over the same trip at the Cheltenham Festival in his first season hurdling. Dan Skelton's four-year-old, who is open to a good deal of improvement after only five starts, will be well suited by the step up to 2m4f this time round and it'll be a big surprise if he doesn't add to his trainer's tally in the coming months. DAN SKELTON

MALONE ROAD (IRE) 6 b g

You have to hand it to Cheveley Park Stud. Whether it's Flat horses or ones for jumping, they rarely get it wrong at the sales. Bought for £325,000 a few months after he won a 3m 4yo maiden point in March 2018, he made a successful rules debut in November of that year before easily following up at Punchestown from a subsequently 142-rated hurdler. He was due to take in the Champion Bumper the following spring but he wasn't seen again due to injury until August 2020, when he bolted up in what was admittedly an ordinary maiden hurdle. Next time his jumping wasn't at his best and he was beaten at long odds on, but it would be folly to write him off after just one run and he remains a horse of great potential. GORDON ELLIOTT.

MAROWN (IRE) 6 b g

Who says the quality of jumpers trained in the North of England is on the decline? Certainly not Nicky Richards, who has won a Scottish National, an Eider and a Grade 1 in Ireland (twice) in recent seasons. The Cumbrian-based trainer has plenty of reasons to be optimistic about another fruitful campaign and we believe his Marown is a horse to follow judging on his progressive and unbeaten profile and the way he has gone about winning his three races. He's essentially a 3m chaser in the making but there are more races to be won with him over hurdles and he's an exciting prospect. NICKY RICHARDS

MENGLI KHAN (IRE) 7 b g

Very useful on the Flat before joining Gordon Elliott, Mengli Khan fairly quickly got the hang of things on his second season hurdling, winning the 2m Grade 1 Royal Bond while still aged four. He didn't manage to add to that in the short term, but was good enough finishing third in the Supreme Hurdle and filled the same position in the Champion Novice Hurdle at Punchestown. A try over fences was next and he got straight off the mark, but after that he couldn't get his head in front for 13 starts, and that was back over hurdles. However, in all that time he was competing in top races, so the opposition was always going to be tough. Prior to his most recent sale, he made all to win a classy 2m3f chase by 26 lengths and is just the type new trainer Nicky Henderson can turn out in all the big Saturday races and festivals. NICKY HENDERSON.

MIDNIGHT CALLISTO 5 br m

It speaks volumes about the regard in which the Anthony Honeyball team hold Midnight Callisto in that they made sure they bought her younger and unraced sister Precious. The five-year-old had a good season in bumpers, winning in fine style at Fontwell by eight lengths. She was sent off favourite for a hot Listed event at Cheltenham and disappointed in eighth with the ground too testing and the run perhaps coming a bit too quick. She was then tested at Listed grade again at Market Rasen but was soundly beaten by Panic Attack, who put in a dazzling performance to win on debut, but that was a solid effort from Midnight Callisto. Her form is strong while she has much more to offer over hurdles. She will be competitive in some nice races against her own sex. ANTHONY HONEYBALL

MINELLA INDO (IRE) 7 b g

Going up in distance has really brought out the best in Minella Indo. An easy winner of a 3m point in March 2018, his first couple of runs for Henry De Bromhead were a bit ordinary, but they were a 2m bumper and 2m4f maiden hurdle. It was the step up to 3m that saw his RPR take a significant rise; the first time was when finishing second to Allaho in a Grade 3. He then took his chance in the Albert Bartlett at the Cheltenham Festival and readily reversed that form at the tasty odds of 50-1. He's since gone on to prove that performance was no fluke, including when sent chasing, and ended his 2019-20 campaign with a second in the RSA, again finishing ahead of his old rival Allaho. A test of stamina is what the son of Beat Hollow relishes and he's expected to be a serious Gold Cup contender in the spring. HENRY DE BROMHEAD.

MONKFISH (IRE) 6 ch g
This physically imposing youngster produced one of the standout novice performances of last season when rallying determinedly to win the Albert Bartlett Novices' Hurdle at the Cheltenham Festival and he has the makings of an even better chaser. The former point-to-point winner is an extremely strong stayer and took a little while to hit top gear last term, improving a fair deal for each start over hurdles. It would appear most likely that the sizeable Stowaway gelding will go novice chasing this year and he makes plenty of appeal as a potential RSA Chase candidate. WILLIE MULLINS

MOSSY FEN (IRE) 5 b g
This five-year-old looked a smart sort over hurdles and is one that is bound to take that next step forward when sent chasing. Before that he won ordinary novice hurdles at Worcester and Aintree and later that year put in a real smart performance to land the Grade 2 Leamington Novices' Hurdle at Warwick. He ran a fine race at the festival when fifth in the Ballymore, again lacking the speed but keeping on resolutely in a very strong

Grade 1 heat. Going chasing and over a longer distance will bring about further improvement, although his hurdle mark of 143 gives connections a few more options in the handicap route. NIGEL TWISTON-DAVIES

NOT THAT FUISSE (FR) 7 b g

A three-time winner over hurdles on good ground earlier in his career, he perhaps failed to make the breakthrough many would have hoped for in novice chases last season. He still ran some excellent races in defeat, finishing second in three of his five outings, including behind Al Dancer at Cheltenham in October, but more often than not was quite convincingly beaten. However, returning as a second-season novice at Perth last month, he created a big impression. He has all the tools required to reach a high level over fences and reportedly is set to be kept away from soft ground this season. He will likely be campaigned with the spring festivals in mind. DAN SKELTON

PALMERS HILL (IRE) 7 b g

This impressive point-to-point winner is still unexposed for the Jonjo O'Neill team but could finally reward connections with a good campaign this year. He has only had two runs in the last two seasons, but both look extremely strong pieces of form. He won a 23-runner handicap hurdle off 124 at Cheltenham's November meeting – beating a horse who bolted up next time out. On his only outing last season, he ran a blinder to finish a neck second in a highly competitive handicap at Kempton. He was beaten by the highly regarded Downtown Getaway, who was well punted on the day, while the third, Our Power, landed a big handicap on his next start. Only raised 4lb, there is plenty of fun to be had with Palmers Hill and as a big, imposing sort he could be campaigned to climb up the handicap ranks over fences. JONJO O'NEILL

PIC D'ORHY (FR) 5 b g

Paul Nicholls has always held this French recruit in the
highest regard and the five-year-old's 33-1 upset in the Betfair
Hurdle didn't seem to come as a huge surprise to the leading
trainer. Connections would have been tempted to supplement
the former Grade 1 runner-up for the Champion Hurdle at
Cheltenham, but bypassing that assignment appears the most
sensible move for his long-term future over fences. Giving him
more time to mature could see him take another step forward
this season and win his share of races. PAUL NICHOLLS

PILEON (IRE) 6 b g

The closing stage of last season's Martin Pipe makes
uncomfortable viewing for anyone who had backed Pileon. For
the Philip Hobbs-trained six-year-old was nailed on the post
by Indefatigable after looking sure to prevail when handed
a decent advantage at the final hurdle. That's not to suggest
there's anything wrong with his attitude – he was just beaten
by a better and more experienced horse on the day – with a gap
back to subsequent Galway winner Great White Shark. He'll be
as effective over a bit shorter and he has the option of either
sticking to hurdles or going chasing. We think he's one to follow,
whichever route he takes. PHILIP HOBBS

PRESENT VALUE (IRE) 6 b g

Another who is interesting as a second-season novice chaser,
Present Value was a tad disappointing last year but certainly
has enough ability to put last season behind him. He has been
an exciting horse since his hurdling days, finishing second to
Al Dancer on his debut before scoring in exciting style next

time out. Over fences last year, he jumped well on his debut when a lengthy second to Champagne Mystery and then ran a decent fourth in a hot-novice race at Exeter. He looked in need of a step up in trip, and over 2m7½f looked to be in control of a decent novice handicap at Newbury. He moved well and jumped excellently, up until the turn for home, making two bad blunders, with the second bringing him down. He is clearly capable of scoring off a mark of 128 and, with a bit more improvement expected, is one that could pick up a bit of a sequence. EVAN WILLIAMS

PRINCESS ZOE (GER) 5 g m

Princess Zoe has potential Grade 1 hurdler written all over her if she's able to translate her Flat ability to obstacles. Talented but showing no signs of being more than average when trained in Germany, she started off with Anthony Mullins on this level with an official mark of 64, but she didn't manage to win off it. However, she then started on a path of rapid progression and held a three-figure mark by the time she won a Listed contest at Galway in September 2020. Other targets on the Flat at the back-end of the season were on the agenda, but it was also said that so long as she schools nicely over hurdles, then she'd be tried over them in novice events, with the ultimate aim of taking her chance at Cheltenham. Good Flat horses don't always excel over timber, but she will take high rank over obstacles if transferring her abilities. ANTHONY MULLINS.

REAL STEEL (FR) 7 b g

While stablemate Al Boum Photo reigned supreme in the Cheltenham Gold Cup, it is worth rewatching how big a run Real Steel had on his first test in a chase over 3m. He travelled into the race superbly, going from the rear on the turn for home to be right in contention and was only a fraction off the leaders at the second last, all the while travelling the widest. But he did not jump the final two with enough enthusiasm and got a little short of room when Santini made his charge. However, it was an impressive effort to finish sixth. He only finished a length behind Delta Work, who dominated the 3m division in Ireland, and he could trouble that rival in those early-season Grade 1 races. It will be interesting to see how far he can go over staying trips this season and whether his master trainer can bring out more improvement. WILLIE MULLINS

RIBBLE VALLEY (IRE) 7 b g

Nicky Richards is a master at giving horses the time they require to develop and the patience he showed last season with this potentially high-class operator is likely to be rewarded this term. The dual bumper winner oozed class when winning pretty manageable assignments at Hexham and Wetherby last November before being sent off 5-4 favourite for a Grade 2 novice hurdle at Ascot the following month. That looked a decent affair but he never seemed himself and failed to really fire in second. He wasn't seen again for the remainder of the campaign. He can prove to be much better than that and add to his tally this time around. NICKY RICHARDS

ROAD SENAM (FR) 4yo b g

As has been stated already, Colin Tizzard houses a classy team of horses, and this season he has Simon Munir and Isaac Souede as part of his owners' group, with their French purchase Road Senam joining the stable. In what may end up being a positive, rather than what might be perceived as a negative, the son of Saint Des Saints never managed a win from seven starts for previous connections, six of those runs at Auteuil. This allows his new trainer to explore all options with his young horse. The other positive is the gelding has already proved he's smart, finishing placed in both Listed and Graded chases, strongly suggesting any ordinary race as a starting point ought to see him get off the mark. We think he's a genuinely exciting prospect. COLIN TIZZARD.

RONALD PUMP 7 ch g

He has done nothing but improve over the last couple of years, progressing rapidly over hurdles from a mark of 102 to 156 in the space of only seven starts. He mixed chasing with hurdling very successfully last season but it was his efforts over hurdles that gained him the most recognition, notably on his final start of the campaign when he finished a tremendous second behind Lisnagar Oscar in the Stayers' Hurdle at the Cheltenham Festival in March. That performance was all the more noteworthy considering he made jumping mistakes and finished with a cut on his leg. He seems to act equally well on good or soft ground and won't be short of big-race options this year, granted his versatility. MATTHEW J SMITH

ROSE OF ARCADIA (IRE) 5 b m

Rose Of Arcadia is another really nice prospect for the Colin Tizzard stable. She's the first horse in training with him wearing the silks of Cheveley Park Stud, who went to £170,000 a few days after she'd landed a 3m soft/heavy-ground mares' point at Tattersalls Farm in Ireland, a race in which the second went on to land her next outing and subsequently join the same Dorset stable. Rose Of Arcadia's sole start in the spring of 2020 saw her trounce her rivals in a Taunton bumper and she may have gone on to contest Graded events later on but the Covid pandemic ended the season. It leaves plans for this year difficult to read, as she could easily remain in bumpers for quite a while to gain more experience or go hurdling. However, we believe there should be plenty more wins. COLIN TIZZARD.

SAINT ROI (FR) 5 br g

There were few more impressive winners at the 2020 Cheltenham Festival than Saint Roi, who bolted up to make a mockery of his opening handicap mark of 137 in the County Hurdle. He has improved markedly for Willie Mullins and has age on his side so it's a distinct possibility he'll turn into a very smart sort over this trip this season. He didn't have to improve to win a Grade 3 in good style at Tipperary on his reappearance in October and, given the lack of strength in depth among the 2m hurdlers, it wouldn't surprise to see him develop into a viable Champion Hurdle contender this season. He'll jump a fence in due course. WILLIE MULLINS

SEBASTOPOL (IRE) 6 b g

Although he's only had five runs since making his rules debut in an Ayr bumper in spring 2018, Sebastopol has shown gradual improvement with each of his five hurdle starts and he posted his best effort when beating several in-form sorts in the Scottish County Hurdle on his final start at Musselburgh in February. This fine-looking son of Fame And Glory was tapped for toe around halfway but came home in good fashion to register a second hurdle victory and a 6lb rise shouldn't be enough to prevent him from winning races this season. Given he has plenty of size and scope, connections also have the option of sending him chasing. TOM LACEY

SHELDON (IRE) 4 ch g

A lesser-known type who would pop up at a bigger price when sent novice hurdling, Sheldon ran a blinder at 50-1 in a very strong Newbury bumper won by Your Darling. He went from racing on the far rail to finishing well on the stands side in the home straight and it is testament to his natural ability that he was able to continue plugging on all the way to the line on testing ground. He disappointed next time at Exeter finishing fourth, but raced a bit too keenly and could just have been feeling the effects of that first run. But Sheldon's first race looked a strong one and he looks open to any amount of improvement when tested over a longer trip and with hurdles in front of him. SEAMUS MULLINS

SHERBOURNE (IRE) 4 b g
There is plenty of expectation in this unraced son of Getaway, who will most likely go novice chasing this year in the colours of Sharp Nicholas and Kennington. He cost £105,000 as a three-year-old and is held in big regard for the season ahead. While he has a big reputation, he has an impressive pedigree to match, being a half-brother to Scottish National winner Joe Farrell. He may be a staying chaser for the future but there is some speed in the family to suggest he could make an impact at novice hurdling level this year. Connections know Getaway well as a sire, having had success last year with The Big Breakaway. COLIN TIZZARD

SHEWEARSITWELL (IRE) 5 b m
Summer jumping form doesn't always translate favourably into winter but this Shirocco mare gave the impression she could be up to mixing it at quite a decent level over hurdles across the coming months with a couple of smart successes since racing resumed. She couldn't have won more easily when strongly supported as 1-2 favourite for a Galway festival bumper in July before showing a substantial engine to strike over hurdles at Sligo the following month, albeit in an ordinary race. She is in the right hands to collect further prizes over the coming months and should be able to make an impact in black type races. WILLIE MULLINS

SHISHKIN (IRE) 6 b g

An impressive winner on his bumper debut, after landing the second of his two outings in points, Shishkin didn't start off his hurdling career in spectacular style at Newbury, falling at the second hurdle having been sent off odds on to beat 19 rivals. Thankfully that was to be the only blip in what was both a progressive and high-class novice season. He returned to the Berkshire track to get off the mark over obstacles 28 days later, pulling 11 lengths clear, and then replicated that exact margin of success when picking up a Listed hurdle at Huntingdon. Just over a month later he took his chance in the Supreme Hurdle, his first attempt in a Grade 1, and he came away with victory by a head from a hugely talented Gordon Elliott-trained horse. He was at the head of the market for the Arkle Chase when this book went to press, so a switch to fences seems his likely route this winter, which should add plenty more wins in his form. NICKY HENDERSON.

SILVER HALLMARK 6 b g

Fergal O'Brien has only managed to get four runs into this smart gelding, but there are plenty of signs that he could be a decent performer over hurdles. He finished a fine third in a red-hot Newbury bumper in March 2019, running on for third behind subsequent Grade 2 winner McFabulous. But it was a different story on his hurdling bow as he reversed the form at Chepstow, jumping impressively, and staying on strongly to win by four lengths. The galloping track played much more into his strengths, and it was a slowly run affair which allowed him to get into his rhythm nicely. He was pitched into the deep end in the Tolworth next time but ran no race, finishing last. That run looked too bad to be true. He could be one to capture some nice prizes over hurdles. FERGAL O'BRIEN

SMURPHY ENKI (FR) 5 b g

He showed some promise in four starts in Irish points as a four-year-old but few could have predicted the ease of this gelding's bumper victory on his debut under Rules at Wincanton in March. Relatively unfancied in the market (14-1), he had plenty of use made of him by Tom Cannon and just went further and further clear of his 11 rivals in the straight, passing the line 18 lengths ahead of his nearest pursuer. It's hard to know what he beat, but it was judged one of the best bumper performances of the season according to RPRs and Song Of Hunter, who'd finished 24 lengths fifth, did come out and win a maiden hurdle at Taunton on his next outing. CHRIS GORDON

SOLO (FR) 4 b g

It was very noteworthy that Paul Nicholls was comparing Solo to the great Master Minded after his first win for the stable at Kempton, but it was no surprise given the impression he made that day in the Grade 2 Adonis Juvenile Hurdle. But Solo ran very poorly when well fancied in the Triumph Hurdle, underperforming in eighth and never in any sort of contention. It is way too early to write him off and it should be noted that the yard ran Frodon and Clan Des Obeaux in this race before they went on to win at Grade 1 level over fences. Chasing is where his future lies but he could be given one more year hurdling and will be interesting when upped in trip. The Grade 1 Prix Renaud du Vivier in France, which Nicholls won with Ptit Zig, would be a good early-season target. PAUL NICHOLLS

SPORTING JOHN (IRE) 5 bb g

Many believed Sporting John could be the horse that could dethrone the mighty Envoi Allen in the Ballymore at Cheltenham but, similar to stablemate Defi Du Seuil, he did not fire at the festival. Philip Hobbs said after the race that he had finished distressed, which makes sense as his performance looked too bad to be true. A line can be drawn through that effort as he had previously shaped as an exceptional prospect, winning back-to-back novice hurdles in fine fashion at Exeter before a very easy win at Ascot in February. Against good yardsticks in Pipesmoker and Master Debonair, he looked in a different league in the way he moved into the race and found plenty at the finish to stretch his advantage. On that form we think he looks one to follow and, as he is still an unknown quantity. He has the look of a chaser and has the point-to-point form if connections decide to go that way. PHILIP HOBBS

ST BARTS (IRE) 6 b g

Another fine chasing prospect for the Philip Hobbs team, St Barts has all the makings of a quality staying chaser for the next few seasons. He could feature in the big winter handicaps in years to come. He only raced four times over hurdles last season, winning an ordinary maiden hurdle at Uttoxeter, but he went on to strike in a nice Ascot handicap in February. He relished the step up to 2m7½f and handled the heavy ground extremely well as he stayed on to the line in good fashion. He is rated 125 which looks well within his compass when conditions are right and he looks bound to progress going over fences. PHILIP HOBBS

STRADIVARIUS DAVIS (FR) 7 b g

Sandy Thompson knows a thing or two about training staying chasers; just have a look at the records of Seeyouatmidnight, Seldom Inn and the hardy Harry The Viking. And the Kelso handler looks to have another potential money spinner on his hands in Stradivarius Davis, who has stepped up considerably on what he achieved over hurdles in his two runs since being switched to Thomson and since switching to fences. He could easily turn out to be the best his trainer has had and he'll be worth looking out for in races like the Rehearsal Chase or the Borders National at the end of the year. SANDY THOMPSON

SULLY D'OC AA (FR) 6 b g

Anthony Honeyball and JP McManus continued their fine
Regal Encore association, last season with Sully D'Oc AA. He
looks capable of capturing a few nice handicaps this season.
The six-year-old did not show too much in four starts last year,
although his Newbury second in November was promising. He
couldn't build on that in his next two starts. His last start was
also encouraging, travelling well but failing to stay in the novice
handicap chase at Cheltenham on Trials Day in January. That
race featured two subsequent festival winners. Going back to
2m may see him in a better light and he could be dangerous
off a mark of 125 when he bounces back to form. ANTHONY
HONEYBALL

THE BIG BREAKAWAY (IRE) 5 ch g

This mighty €360,000 purchase was bred to be a chaser and
is hopefully going to fulfil his potential this season. He did
very little wrong when warming up over hurdles, winning
in emphatic fashion in two fairly strong novice heats at
Chepstow and Newbury. Although he was sent off 1-2 on the
latter, it looked a strong race with the second, Papa Tango
Charly, costing a fortune. He shaped well when fourth in the
Ballymore. Going up to 3m and over fences is exactly what he
needs and connections believe he could reach the peak of that
division this season. His schooling is reportedly exceptional.
COLIN TIZZARD

THE BIG GETAWAY (IRE) 6 b g

Last season's Ballymore Novices' Hurdle at Cheltenham may
end up being very strong form in the coming months so The
Big Getaway, third in that contest, is definitely one for this
book. A 30-length winner of a point before making his rules
debut, he didn't make an immediate impact in bumpers but
got off the mark at the third attempt before going hurdling.
Trainer Willie Mullins has said in the past that this son of

Getaway is as big as any horse he's ever had, which suggests that while we've already seen he's got a massive engine, he's going to keep progressing with age. He shaped like the best in the field for much of his first start over hurdles, in what was a hot race, but didn't quite see it out. He then bolted up Naas. That aforementioned final start at Cheltenham confirmed his high level of ability and he shapes as though he might be a bit special over fences. WILLIE MULLINS.

THE BOSSES OSCAR (IRE) 5yo b g

On jumping the penultimate hurdle of last season's Martin Pipe at the Cheltenham Festival, The Bosses Oscar, who hadn't travelled with much fluency, only had four of the 23-strong field behind him. However, Gordon Elliott's five-year-old finished to such effect that he managed to bag fifth place, beaten less than four lengths on only his fourth start over hurdles. That effort in conjunction with his pedigree bolsters the view that he'll be even more effective as he goes up to 3m and it wouldn't be any surprise to see him try to break the stranglehold of his stable companion Sire Du Berlais in the Pertemps Final over that trip at the festival. GORDON ELLIOTT

THE CON MAN (IRE) 7 b g

Donald McCain and owner Tim Leslie experienced the pleasure of dining at the top table with both Peddlers Cross and Overturn, both Grade 1 hurdle winners, earlier this century. And, although things have been quieter for the pair at the highest level in recent seasons, The Con Man looks just the sort to make up into a smart hurdler and/or novice chaser in the coming months. This progressive triple hurdle winner, who won his sole start in points, shapes as though the step up to 3m will suit and, as he's only had six outings. There's almost certainly more to come from this scopey sort. DONALD MCCAIN

THIRD TIME LUCKI (IRE) 5 b g

Dan Skelton has quickly established himself as one of the top National Hunt trainers and he has a promising hurdler for the upcoming season in Third Time Lucki. The five-year-old showed he had a serious engine when bolting up in bumpers at Market Rasen and at Huntingdon in winter and, although he couldn't extend the winning run in the Champion Bumper at Cheltenham, he showed improved form to finish fourth behind Ferny Hollow. Given the way he finished that day he'll be equally at home over further when he goes over hurdles and this highly regarded sort is sure to make his mark in that new discipline. DAN SKELTON

THYME HILL 6 b g

It feels like Thyme Hill should be a more recognised name than he currently is. A six-length winner on his first ever start, which was in a Worcester bumper, connections were clearly keen to step their horse up in company quickly, as he then finished a neck second in a Listed event before claiming third in the Champion Bumper. He won a Grade 2 on his opening try over hurdles. Another race at that level came next before he picked up the Grade 1 Challow Hurdle as an odds-on shot. He lost his unbeaten status over timber when upped in distance to 3m for the Albert Bartlett, but looked unlucky there, and emerged with his reputation intact. As a six-year-old, there is a chance he might go chasing but if he stays over the smaller obstacles, he can be a leading player for the Stayers Hurdle in March considering he appears to enjoy his trips to the Cheltenham Festival. PHILLIP HOBBS.

TIME FLIES BY (IRE) 5 ch g

Time Flies By took little time to introduce himself as a top prospect when an impressive winner of a strong bumper at Cheltenham on just his second start. Over hurdles he never quite lived up to expectations, finishing third in the Grade 2 Supreme Trial at Ascot and then well beaten again in the Ballymore trial. He did, however, move well into the race but his effort in the closing stages was disappointing. Although his only win came on heavy ground he may prefer conditions to be slightly better. Also his four starts were in quick succession, which could be another excuse for his drop in form. It will be interesting to see what the handicapper does to give connections more options over hurdles. The Martin Pipe, which JP McManus is usually well represented in, may be an interesting long-term target. NICKY HENDERSON

TUPELO MISSISSIPPI (IRE) 5 b g
Brian Ellison and owners Phil and Julie Martin have been associated with several classy animals including Definitly Red, Forest Bihan and Windsor Avenue. The same team has another potentially decent sort in Tupelo Mississippi, who progressed nicely in bumpers following an encouraging debut second in an Irish point. Tupelo Mississippi bolted up on Newcastle's all-weather before showing a fine attitude to follow up under a penalty on the same track's turf course just before the national lockdown in March. He'll be suited by the step up to 2m4f when he goes over hurdles and he has the physique to make a chaser in time. BRIAN ELLISON

YOUR DARLING (IRE) 5 b g
It was fascinating to hear Ben Pauling speak so highly of Your Darling after his debut win in a warm bumper at Newbury. The performance itself was exciting enough, as he moved smoothly and stayed on quite well in very heavy conditions at Newbury. He also toppled hot favourite Flinteur Sacre (mentioned above in this publication), brother to Sprinter Sacre, who obliged next time out to boost the form. It all went wrong next time out but a line can be drawn through that as he remains a leading

prospect over hurdles. Remember, the Pauling-trained Barters Hill beat Buveur D'Air and Altior in a Newbury bumper so the trainer's high praise is certainly worth noting. BEN PAULING

YOUNG LIEUTENANT (IRE) 6 b g
Another who can take advantage in a second season as a novice hurdler, Young Lieutenant looked like a winner in waiting when a runner-up at Newbury on his first start. He proved no match for the strong-travelling Sir Valentine but did everything right and kept on well. But the wheels came off from there where he seriously underperformed in four outings since. He has shaped up as if he would improve for a step up in trip, while the heavy ground looked far from ideal on his last few runs. The wind surgery and summer break may have done him the world of good and a mark of 122 could allow him to climb up the handicap ladder. His trainer has always rated him as a top prospect and we do too. WARREN GREATREX

INDEX

100 WINNERS
HORSES TO FOLLOW FLAT 2021

Companion volume to **100 Winners: Jumpers to Follow**, this book discusses the past performances and future prospects of 100 horses, selected by Raceform's expert race-readers, that are likely to perform well on the Flat in 2021.

To order post the coupon to the address below or order online from **www.racingpost.com/shop**
Tel 01933 304848

ORDER FORM

Please send me a copy of **100 WINNERS: HORSES TO FOLLOW FLAT 2021** as soon as it is published. I enclose a cheque made payable to Pitch Publishing Ltd for **£6.99** (inc p&p)

Name (block capitals) ....

Address ....

....

Postcode ....

SEND TO: PITCH PUBLISHING,
SANDERS ROAD, WELLINGBOROUGH, NORTHANTS NN8 4BX [100F21]

NOTES